REID THE WORDS
Derek Reid

These poems were written between 1968 and 2022

All rights reserved. No part of this publication may be reproduced, stored in a retrieval system or transmitted, in any form, or by any means, electronic, mechanical, photocopying, recording or otherwise, without the prior permission of the author.

This book is sold subject to the condition that it shall not, by way of trade or otherwise, be lent, resold, hired out or otherwise circulated without the author's prior consent in any form of binding or cover other than that in which it is published and without a similar condition being imposed on the subsequent purchaser.

Copyright © Derek Reid 2023

ISBN: 9798371859549

ACKNOWLEDGEMENTS

Phil Lawder (Poet and writer who helped me put this collection together)
Pinner Poets (for their encouragement)
The Society for Storytelling (promoting the oral tradition of storytelling)
Oscar Tapper (Poet and Editor of East London Arts Magazine - ELAM in 1960s)
The Teachers of Upton House Secondary School

INDEX

A Candle Burns	8
On The Subject of Light	10
Storyteller	11
Song After Solomon	13
The Testament of Memory	14
At the Café in Golders Hill Park	16
A Minute of Your Time, Perhaps	18
Yiddish Song and Klezmer Music	20
Wishful Thinking	22
For Stella, Rachel and Ben	24
He Saw a Hundred Deaths on the Ceiling	25
Christmas Night	26
A Boxing Day Meet	28
The Grave Digger Speaks	30
The Muluch Ha'Movez	32
After Euridice	34
England, She Dances	35
Soul Speech	36
On the Death of a Friend	37
' stood Today	38
Going Home	39
In the Silence of the House	40
Oscar Perry Tapper	41
August Ends	42
Grand Hotel	43
Somewhere, Some Time	44
War Song of the Love Bed	45
Bedroom Seen	46
Water Babies	47
But It's True	51

Voices of Spring	53
He is a Hairdresser to Ladies	54
Touches of Love	55
Working Script	57
On my Seventieth Birthday	58
The Shaman's Dance	60
Lizzie Strade	63
Cabaret Song	65
Gurney at the Words	67
With Apologies to William Allingham	69
Nightmare	70
I Wake	71
Tisha B'AV	72
Blackbury Castle (1)	75
Blackbury Castle (2)	76
Why Poetry?	77
To the Storytellers	78

To my family for their belief in storytelling and song:

"Booba" Annie & "Zider" Raphael (grandparents)
Sylvia & Alf (parents)
Neil and **Raina** (brother and sister)
Pippa (wife)
Abigail (daughter)
Rachel & Ben & Stella (daughter, son-in-law and granddaughter)

Avraham Nahum Stencl ("The Rav", Yiddish poet and my mentor)

A Candle Burns

A candle burns for those forgotten,
for those who've passed and passed and gone,
for those who've passed beyond the stage of memory,
bore the thought we'd bring them home.

Through stories told to me by elders
I've heard "the hep!" and felt the flames,
hid from mobs in time of pogrom,
done to death in a Greco-Hebrew name.

The gods of old begat my coming,
I have walked eternity,
out of Eden, through its jungle of becoming,
 I am myself the refugee.

There is no earth where I've not wandered,
desert, plain, and city street
met the eyes that you've averted,
tasted hunger, sensed disbelief.

Akin to death is how I'm pictured,
skin and bone with haunted eyes,
my colour's black and white and browning,
your clothes I wear are not my size.

Do I believe you are my brother?
You will forgive me if I say,
that I have heard that said so often,
its meaning lessens every day.

There is hatred in each country,
persecution ignites fear,
rich versus poor and vice versa,
the immigrant and people here.

We've come a long way from the garden
walking forward, looking back,
diverged to many trackways
and lost the route to have the knack.
A simple thought, this world's for sharing,
how many times I've heard that said,
but what is meant by shared is different
they that share the earth in unity
are the speechless, who are dead.

A simple thought, too simple maybe,
is as we circle round looking forward
to the garden, the trees of Eden lie behind us
in the forests of our minds.....waiting to be found.

On the Subject of Light

It is here on this street, this straight solid strand
of concrete, stone, glass and hubbub in the hours
either side of midnight that light and dark confront
themselves and each other, attempting to merge
each into the other like lovers, like lovers
it is not allowed of them and so they kiss in closeness
and stand off.

'mid loose words, anger, love songs, laughter
and incessant chatter lights change,
there are whispers and cold undercurrents,
built blocks characterless of unimagined learning
over-shadowing a tale of Gothic masonic
engineering, to bring even the dead eye
back to life.

All ages sleep here, blanking the showy neons
ancient and be-whiskered old folk and friends,
busy young Troglodytes cave in inset doorways,
feet from a feast of storage in a space of supposed waste,
each inset a step down to the lower depths -
hell here is the cold and the chatter of teeth
with nothing to say.

On this street, I notice a common similarity
and a difference as in many places
in this world, light whatever its source
flattens and obscures, whilst the darkness
illuminates, light gives birth to shadows,
whilst the cloaking dark is the coverall
for feelings.

Storyteller

Somewhere in his head seventy half-forgotten languages
he learnt before birth, form and reform in a floating space
of ribbon themes borne on warm thoughts
and fleeting images, he glimpses and grasps
and clasps to find absent in the open palm
of a mind's arm, as time's sand licks its fingers.

His coloured tongue, coat grey tablet-like and ancient
without being, he has loved a thousand times,
held his love, lived with her, she of many faces,
kissed and watched her go, dissolving where he takes her.
god-like were he, who with words gave her creation,
stationed her to sleep on the bed of his mouth.

He is the lifetime child-man, self soul born of earth
a titan whose brain conceives, whose mouth gives birth,
fully formed he draws his children through his lips
out into a wordy world where against the Tartarus dark*
they are the spark that lights the moonlit minds of man,
all this he can do before devouring them.

He, like the poet, pains and speaks a divine affliction,
walks beside us spelling hells and paradise like a prophet
and knows not why his gift was given or the curse was laid.
He sees to tell it is his must – but as do the dead fold into the landscape
he escapes us, his face falls away, and from his words hang memory,
and seventy languages have spawned the carriage of a thousand tongues.

There is an ancient Midrashic legend which tells amongst many things that during the period between conception and birth the child foetus is taught how it's life will span; it will be taught to speak seventy languages; what and who it will be. This legend also contained an explanation of the phenomenon known as Déjà vu

Song After Solomon

And she loved her love
like the Shulamite
as she held him close
to dreams
he fed on her words
and majesty
and she clustered at his seams.

Her breath was that
of honey-dew
and he sipped the sweet
within
her love was love
and plenty
and he made his bed therein.

Night has likened
to the ruby
love tongues,
the dart of light
like flames
they flicker brightly
in the fires of night.

And their love was earth
and mountain
was foundation
and the sky –
such is love
which is eternal
that is built upon a sigh.

The Testament of Memory   (For Shonaleigh)

I am older than the hills
And younger than tomorrow:
I was there the first Friday after time,
The first Friday of the world.

I saw the garden
And broke the ground,
Helped build a tower, saw it
Tongue-tied tumbling.

' was taken up to talk to God -
' still do.
My route is marked by storytellers –
From the Ta'nach – Torah, Nevi'im, Kesuvim,
        (The 5 Books of Moses, The Prophets & other items)

Haggadah, Aggadah, Megillot,
Through Gamaliel, Hillel, Akiva, and Strength* the son of bitterness;
The Tanna'im, the Talmidayhem, and Rashi
who influenced every story tradition in Europe (or was influenced
by it).

The Chabad of Nachman of Bratizslav,
And the folkies – Mendel Mocher Seforim, Sholem Aleichem,
Peretz, Anski, my laughter and tears. They set my hand to the page
for fear of losing one story amongst the nations.

A thousand years have passed since my brother Ishmael called mine
"The people of the book".

By words, deeds and wingless angels
Have I numbered the signs and portents;
By hirsute sleeve and bravo coat*. Aye and the dreamers!
Where would I be without my dreamers in those days of soulless dark?

From the dream of father Adam I have seen it all,
From beginning to end...the flowers of Meggido –
I have seen it all and until I am ready
Yom Ha'Din (The Day of Judgement) will wait.

Strength son of bitterness ...a very interesting folk image drawn from the name Jesus (Joshua) son of Mary. More a seemingly symbolic reference to rebellion that to an actual person at the time of difficulties with Rome.

By hirsute sleeve and bravo coat! Refers to Jacob and Joseph

At the Café, Golders Hill Park

By appointment an outpost of the Vienna Woods
with youth hurled back over half a century
and more of them in memory than the ache
to climb the hill.

Perhaps it would be best by the easy way
dropped by car at the top and the colours
of the pond and the gardens left to lie
for Summer and the disturbance of music, a band,
and the crowd, but there would be a missing ache
something less to talk around to noise a grumble.

These people brought their summer here long ago
the stretched hump of a deckchair sages
half asleep in the communicating lilt of language
Strauss spoke at a different time. Most ancients here
hold the same ancestry as Strauss.

Most at many times have lived
more lives than one as shadow on the street,
as new name with a foreign utterance
a spelling if not changed, re-named.

Dapper with old world courtesy, steepled fingers
extended cuffs, bald chin and naked pate
an old man teaches a girly circle
eight decades deep in make-up, how
he would make strudel. They listen, they let him dream.

My coffee smiles and I take in
its breaths as children of affluence gather
always mouthing for more
always loudly wanting!

It was like this then when young.
They put distance to their past and were part
of their Vienna – conservative, radical,
as Jewish as memory would make them mannered
as proper as Roses from the South.

I drain the last flavour, regard another old man and his listeners,
take in the philosopher holding a choice of chess pieces in his blind fists.
He is for a war of the mind – death will stalk his summer and he will laugh,
his ache will be exasperation but he will put it down with words.

And I will spend my Summer Sunday mornings
on the fringes of my faith here,
dancing by appointment on the tongues
of the old, in this outpost of the Vienna Woods.

Strauss refers to Austrian composer Johann Strauss II
'Roses from the South' a waltz written by him.

A Minute of Your Time, Perhaps?

A minute of your time perhaps?
The hour that we have?
A cup of tea, a biscuit and a story.
The lady with the brimming eyes
Whose soul was in her face,
Offered little but her recent months of worry.
Widowed once, she'd met a man
A music man at that,
Whose strengths were there ever to support her,
A teller and a doer, he was the one
                    to always know
But he wouldn't live the ills, to suffer slowly.

If there's something you would give
Let it be time, let it be time –
For the future's in the past
But for the telling.
It's the silver on the glass
That's the difference in extent
Between your window on the world
And that you dwell in.

And the world in so much hurry
It has no time to hear
The feeble voice that carries with it aging.
The old man stirred reflections
On the surface of his cup
Whilst his eyes are sunk within him disengaging.
Once he was a boy, he was a man,
He was the world
And that staircase rang with tumult and his children,
Now his children's children do not give him time of day,
They the losers in the silence he is leaving.

18

I sing the generations
Of the songlines across time,
A tying-to of elderly and infant.
The story that is handed on
To make the living worth
the sharing of harmonious contentment.
I remember, I remember
And the vagrant's "poor life this"
If to take the time to listen we are losing,
Then the obvious end to everything is loneliness itself
On a sphere in which (so we're told), communication's booming!

The first tears on a telling
Held in check for forty years
I have witnessed
as an old man worked up to them –
And all the myths and magics
through which children conjure life
On a road of growing darkness for the tragic.
So put the stories up and let them live between our ears
Let us hear and ride excitement in the learning.
If in giving time to others we teach others how to hear
Then at least we will be part of someone's story.

If there's something you would give
Let it be time, let it be time –
For the future's in the past
But for the telling.
It's the silver on the glass
That's the difference in extent
Between your window on the world
And that you dwell in.

Yiddish Song & Klezmer Music (*Dus iz in'zer'ra**)
(dedicated to my friend, colleague and musician, Joel Rubin)

I will now try (as the magician says)
"The near impossible trick" of translating an emotional sound
into the flattened excitement of words on a page,
and a voice in vibrating air. But
the purpose of words is limitation,
whilst music expands. The like of you and I
listen here with hope to understand but feel the music
where the speechless heart ethereally sings, soars
in revelation and plummets darkly to express desolation.

The music of my folk is inward prayer
and exaltation, a murmur to the universe and a shout
to its enclosure, an ingratiating sway, and a swaggering thanks
to the force that stands behind me, the thou of respect
and the you of a friend. I am at home, at heart,
in the arms of my forebears, and in the laps of generating mothers
I can be the child I was here in the songs
and instrumentations, where I have lived,
loved, lost and won – before and in my time.

Roumanische, Polishe, outcast of empires,
and artistes of their intellectual traditions, indeed singers to kings,
soloists to orchestras, conversationalists to creativity
and like my uncle Esau, father of the Rom, an egging smile
to encouraging achievements. In the hanging tears of crochets,
and the reflective sighs of quavers, I had hung out of me
who I am indeed long before I learnt to speak.
Songs of my folk, of my family, solo or in harmony
caressed my infant consciousness and I settled to a learning.

I remember old men who pinched my cheek
and chucked my chin laughing as I answered in giggles,
who gathered in halls, home, and old world restaurants
who played (I thought) just for me. I grew, they gathered dust,
their music kitsched and commercialised almost to oblivion.
Then the voice of the child three generations on somewhere,
asked "That tune you're la-la-ing, where does it come from...,
and is it one of ours.....and can you teach it to me?"
And so we who held the memory, cried with joy in silence
and smiled in our hearts.

Note: The words Dus iz in'zer'ra (This is ours) should be read to mean the possessive.

Wishful Thinking

The night sky is jewelled by the light of the stars
millions of miles away, some of those seen
extinguished have been, but appear like a dream
by delay, the twinkle of shine that catches the mind,
that illuminates love and desire science tells us, is caused
by a break or a pause in a wavelength of light that transpires.

But what if it's not? What if we've got a pressure
of human design, an invisible source
of such immensely great force intensely
produced by a want of the mind.
A thought borne aloft but by science struck off,
scoffed, as a concept the moonstruck defined.

Imagine, I ask, that through centuries past how many
have wished on the stars, and the weight of those wants
requesting response have added their gravity plus
arising unseen by us as extreme, by those others as where
their love starts, and what interferes in the light
of spent years, is the winging of wishes between.

Science has said that some stars appear dead
with the weight of a gravitational force,
so crushed they implode under invisible loads
collapsing to create inner space, turned inside out
they are gateways of doubt, where love and light
are burnt out negative vacuums and new universes formed.

Algebraic equations and a wish are evasions
the longings of love, peace, lust and empires
all hang here, fearing the silenced time of eternities
on the rationale of want and the absence of discerning light,
both seek a solid answer where all that's substantial
is constantly destroyed, and therefore does not yet or since exist.

Suicide's pits and soul eating despondency suck
through the shapeless pained anguish of an emptiness,
burning black holes darkly through matter, where empty ends
and tortured beginnings are turned in upon themselves,
and one big bang can smash such plains
and thousands more can this endlessly create.

For Stella, Rachel and Ben

As family we saw you coming from a long way off
your being illuminating our conversation
like the stars at a distance, we could not help
but notice you.

Even at a distance in the dark of unknowing
you shone and lit up our conversation,
word was that with your new light
shades paled

You arrived like song – a sweet starlight giver
and in your own way brought welcome
as in wide eyed and wonder filled
pure personality

Star gazing deeply into our welcome souls
the question of Who? Why? and What?
lie as future landscapes seen, surveyed,
stumbled on.

What we pour on you is love above all,
and shower words and mouth the marvel
of your being something so small
and new to us.

Star child of a patient wait, far far have you come
on the space seed of love, you are asking
already. We see questions already
Stella, star brightness your shining has begun.

(Our granddaughter Born 29th January 2021)
Written 12/03/2021

He Saw a Hundred Deaths on the Ceiling

He saw a hundred deaths on the ceiling
at the edges of his vision, he scrolled the calendars
forward and back, whilst the screens
the upright rectangles at the centre of his sight
took him as fast as he wished across the years.
Here was history coming and gone, names
yet to be, pauses, partings, moving pictures.
Sometimes whilst all this occurred a girl's head,
never the same one, appeared over a date on the calendar page to ask
if there was anything he desired. His answer was always no
it was enough to see all this
and see himself seeing it all.

All this time his eyes were closed to the world
his mind shut off – sight unseen
but he was in there and active.

Christmas Night
(Dedicated with her permission to my great friend and Morris Dancer, Janet Dowling)

Christmas night, I slept on a pillow of thoughts,
tumbling through a mind field, to wake
in the dark to the scatter language and laughter, to the whistle
of command and the odd and brittle tinkle of attending bells.

I thought for a moment my reason's tumble had turned
such considerations to tears of self torture,
but then my eyes were opened, to wake me wider in that dark
and my tears were sweat and dew from a mossy ground.

Beside my bed a ribbon of mud and puddles ran
and from somewhere in mind memory prompted me
to recall it was the Menin Road, a walk of dead men -
recall! Falling into slumber in my time I had been elsewhere.

False lightening brought my mind to bear, here! Now!
The ever present! The percussion of the guns,
the shrieking whistles, the fall and flattened thud hums,
and the sound of feet in rhythm, coming on in unison.

Somewhere up front history sacrificed soldiers
to death, whilst that angel did the round dance of battles.
Somewhere behind me the feet that I'd heard, were
nearer me now, but they bore not the sloven shuffle of cattle.

Lightness of foot marked their advance, a lightness
once heard then remembered, the men of the shires
would be dancing tonight in practice
for the twenty-sixth of December.

England alive! Saint George and the rest. They did not dance
to the drum, but to whistles and songs with great laughter,

four lines of four men, two sets and an officer who
was dressed to play bagman and fool.

How once they crashed stick on stick and stung their palms
in mockery of hunting, now rifle butt to rifle butt
their reef of smiles like moonlit bunting
they beat the war cry of a nation knowing not to what they hastened.

The slapping clash of the catching hand, its sound
like the firing bolt driven home, the laughter then
of these happy men will forever fill my ears as will commands
to cross, re-cross and strip the willow.
I sat and wept to watch them go, knowing how the villages
would miss them, I knowing of the silence they would leave behind
and the generations that would bless them, knowing too their dance goes on
where their village young still wish it.

Somehow I saw the fate that awaited, where the music would stop
and the laughter fall away, where the moon of the darkness
would be clouded by debris and grey cannon smoke
rob them of their day. A whistle I heard as they found their history -
One blast, six words, the voice of their captain spoke "Men of The Shires - Dance on!".

Somewhere upon a foreign field a team, a ghost army
of ancient English dancers are drawn up by the rising sun,
to dance out for our Summer. They rise up like the grass of Spring,
who were cut down before their time, and chant with us the chants they gave
who dance forever beyond the grave.

A Boxing Day Meet

Saint Stephen's Day cold and the Mummers are loose,
Death and rebirth happen today
Whilst you curl here little brother,
Elsewhere in the country
They are tearing your cousins to pieces
English dogs and mad men,
But you idle time in a suburban garden
You know where is your greatest safety
Right under your enemy's eyes,
safe in his heart.

Seemingly asleep for long periods of time
But aware and itchy at sounds
Raising yourself to groom and curling down again.
From the sky the crows call, about you the circling
jays land, sidle up hopping, skipping,
Backing off, away from an unseen force field of fear.
Strut and pull back, circle, strut and pull back.

And yet you lie – allowing them their space
Their warlike spiral of probing dance.

Up in my eyrie, I am positioned to look down on you
Yet I see you sense my presence
An Olympian on whom you have bestowed
the pleasure stillness...I am invisible
Even to you caged as I am beyond the glass,
Embodied in houses. Small, for that you are
We carry a mystique, an aura that tells you
We are about.

Reynard my brother, slip away now
like the doze you have just taken – go now in peace,

Be brave, be brave, but not too brave!

The Grave Digger Speaks

I've seen the grave from the inside
and the out, in a manner o' speakin'.
In a way I speak to God
every day and he don't mind
the occasional swear word,
whilst I'm workin'.
Because of his closeness
because of his closeness
I sometimes think he must swear
because I hear him breathin'
in exasperation as he picks out of the hole,
the hollows of the unused years.

Ghosts! I don't believe in 'em
'cause if you don't know it
the soul goes on forever, sure
a new face every time – most
times a vague memory of place
and people. He, she,
it may wear a difference each
oncoming next time they return.
Yer know we're never quite finished.
We lose something of the memory
and returned like library books
and birthdays, we are like birthday candles,

Waxed, illuminating, spirit lights.
There's an old legend of the ancients,
about the smallest bone at the top of the spine,
at the bottom of the skull that
whenever everything else is gone he
comes back for it! It's the key, that's his key
for a slight re adjustment after you

think you're finished, when you think
you have stopped thinking,
he reprogrammes a hundred languages
appoints a sole entity to educate you
because you howl out of loss,
language gone....and somebody else.

The Muluch Ha'Movez. Thoughts on a Companion
(Hebraic title for the soul collector, The Angel of Death)

Today, tomorrow,
he has my name on his tongue,
the hocked and hobbling angel.

First or last he will fill his pockets
with the seams of life, the loose
broken threads torn of a moment.

Hanging over the edge of a pocket
of his ancient overcoat;
knotted and splayed
in eyelashes
of prayer fringes.

How many times has he
passed me in a day
and touched my heart, for his reassurance.

My pains he will consign
to an inside pocket
or even, maybe
his ever empty, bottomless
wallet.

He is without faith,
he knows the boss
and the prophets, their shares
in the futures market,
being the last, it is he
who will laugh the loudest.

He is an old friend
who throws the cartoon carpet
of his shadow before me
and we share the joke,
because he throws no shadow.

But not even for him
will I fall down once
on my face
like a clown.

When the time comes
I will answer to his smile
and his guiding arm
around my shoulders.
It will be his joke
and I will lift my shoulders,
raise my eyes, sigh,
and drop my eyelids
and smile
all in resignation.

After Eurydice

Love and death,
Sheet music,
Even they
Play out in silence!

I turned and she
    Was gone!
No shade, no shadow,
Swiped from the page,

A caged interval of interminable length.

I had taken my mind
Off her for an instant
To gain sight, but it came
And went and gave me nothing.

Now I am bits and pieces
Torn apart and living moments
I am one with the howling wind
Mouth to mouth, our song is all echoes
And soul searching

England, She Dances (for Abigail)

Sun up, and star fall,
the first of May.
The Flowers of dance are a-field,
are a-forest, calling on nature
to dance up the sun, to flourish full light,
now winter is done. The petals of beauty
wave breezy their white linens
at dawn, the word songs
of morning, the fiddle of light,
the birdsong of England
see the last of gruff winter's night –
calling on spirits who have slept in the mists
and the aged ageless legends
Of story who will once more
come to exist.

Soul Speech

The time of youth it has fair faces
I remember many do,
together in their time and places,
first names unchange, unlined the smiles I knew.

I see them still without aging traces
years ago and to this day
memories I carry with me
for slow moments as I grey

Who and why and for what reason
the call of souls all worlds away
the sound of voices far beyond me
take me back to learning days

I see them all my crowd of faces
some I know no longer here,
I greet them all as they live with me,
perhaps where they exist I too appear?

Tomorrow never comes they tell me
but yesterday is always here,
As the poet I remember all the times
we shared that brought me here.

How many times the clock has tolled me
passed his hand across my eyes,
passed a present in that darkness
beyond this life, where what's future lies.

When the time comes they'll come with me,
memories of all I knew, and perhaps
in time they will tell me
how they felt when I they knew.

On the Death of a Friend   (Barry)

His sister, I, and another,
the nurse encouraged us to call out to him
to shout!
    to call him back.
Back from the outward journey, from the space
he sought, in absenting himself
in timelessness across the soundless void.

Something carried for a farewell smile
curled his lips, and touched colour to his cheeks,
but from across this moving distance
his last wave registered
in the pain of a grimace, and twitches
that flicked off the switches of living.
His last breath not done like a padded footfall
heard through a closing door,
drew from us a slow intake
almost as if we would hold something
of his being close, in some part of what?

Those twitches also showed recognition,
for the life of him
he was not coming back.
Like hailing folk on a shoreline cliff
after a passing coaster,
our loudness was diminished by the distance.
Our words met echoes and absorption,
we could not stop him, he was moving away-
further than thought, further than fading features.
Thought had caught him on the stair,
tripped him on his journey on a strand of if
and if not? - Could be done?
'don't think so!

' stood Today

' stood today with a young mum where the bus stops along
Westminster Road
on the Wyche, on its downhill journey to the bustle.
We said nothing across a moment of years,
The years between us but a book of breezes
here fanning the heat of the day with memory.
Separated by age and inches, seeing
but not seeing,
Shadows by incident light, objects of peripheral vision
Perhaps though aware
each of the other, something at the time
Together, our backs to the road
We looked out across the drape of landscape -
this hill's well of ancient heady wine and green magic.
I sensed a fear in what she saw and set the image to my mind.
The music in my ears was aircraft drones
And the wind that has always sung the trees here,
And the wind that has always sung the trees here swelled
lifted and took from us the mechanical sound.
For her they were gone to the city. For me it was just good they
were past.
I felt her question on the air,
Caught in the corner of my eye the slight turn of the head, seeking,
I thought for a moment, her man who she missed most of all –
How did I know that?
Head still turning with a question of eyes she whispered
The one name only folks * used for me.
I was her future,
She brought me here
She smiled and when I thought to answer her "Mum?"
Then time and the light stood us apart, and I heard only
the echo of her in the wind, the wind
that has always sung the trees here. *close family*

Going Home

They're going home like the good shoes that they are
they're going home, perhaps after one more journey,
and perhaps
one more beyond that? They're going home
like us they don't last forever.

They're going home like the good shoes that they are
they've come a long way miles and miles of overbearing,
and definitely
worn in and worn out
by the tread of my weight.

They're going home like the good shoes that they are
they're going home, scuffed and scarred and equally
unpresentable
rough as the year, impish in appearance
as a prickly youth stubble struck.

They're going home to retire green to the garden,
they've come a long way having tasted so much of the earth
I'll grant them the peace
and a place in my nostalgia,
they're coming home to reminisce, we three.

In the Silence of the House

In the silence of the house
after the hubbub of breakfast,
I see him, my father, in his last days,
sitting on the settee
in the corner of the dining room,
flipping through a day's broadsheet
like the calendar of a life
that will not come again.

He laughs at small tales
of the moment and as quickly
as they entertain, they pass,
Resigned, the world
is no longer his problem
though seeds of his concern
are planted in the furrows
of his thoughts.

He is not here, but I see him
as solid as he always was,
and somewhere in my head
the quiet rarity of his
singular laugh strikes me -
he turns his face to me, grins
"Anything I can help with boychick?"
And I kiss the whisper "Pops!"

Oscar Perry Tapper

Falstaff to my Hal,
he lived in France
under the shadows of giants
and a castle. In London by the gate
the Old or Aldgate
near to The Tower. In both
by the river,
and the crowded market,
in both, loving. A mischievous
lord of misrule, a Bacchus
of belly and laughter,
a teacher of wisdom
and fun.
From the Lion D'Or
he saw his London. In London
Chinon was forever
on his lips.

August Ends / Setting Sun, September
(Thoughts on the substance of Nostalgia)

September comes and I sit sunning myself,
a solitary on a park bench, aware
of the lengthening shadow and the cooling
of its shade, thinking darkly of the stack of years
my pockets hold. So much said to so many faces
hooked by questions of forgotten names,
times and places, to so many faces
hooked by marks of question
to forgotten names,
times and places still remembered.
How many times have I ever lost it?
them? Individuals and laboured in fascination
of when they slipped away, out of focus, out of frame,
lost in name, hugs and heartaches those heavy weathers,
hurt by loss and hung enquiries - tablets taken
to forget a pain: The wanton body that I held at arms' length,
whose classic mystique crumbled
through its pregnant time.
The lie of sex, the love of women,
the cause of hurt, the harm in a moment's grace.

The sea of faces and sojourning places – older folk,
family before me, gone. I sit here sitting solely, soully
re-creating in recreation. Passing time for its hour
in dying light for a little more illumination.

Grand Hotel

Shades of Empire, rosy shadows
Ghostly, Roses from the South,
Waltz dreams, fans and invitation dances,
Programme ticks, palm court romances;
But now too few strings play your salon music
And ladies are withdrawn into their shade,
The ballroom fills for those who can remember,
As everything that did begins to fade.

Claret days and dinner brandies
Memoirs, in they flittered past,
Distance stretched out anti clockwise
Already gone, the moment dies;
But now too few strings play your salon music
The terrace is a place that love neglects,
And words that ran like rivers from dark corners
Lie cooling in nostalgic retrospect.

Frail lady, light as chiffon
The gentleman behind "The Times",
Thought waves surge and burst their ages
Wiping time from aging pages;
But now too few strings play your salon music
And high tea is not taken on the lawn
Two days ago so quickly is forgotten
And love's sweet song will die this coming dawn.

Somewhere, Some Time

Somewhere on its run the river of time races rapids
unsettled by some stones as it meanders along,
life can hold you up or can drag you through the shallows -
emotions can tie you down if you don't think that you're strong.

Time and tide they'll tell you you must question every answer
you must have the fullest answers when others opinionate
for every soul is different, every story has beginning
and the ending of each telling is the rolling out of fate.

It's only the lack of vision that is blind love in the seeing
is the ignoring of some small hurts in the know,
is the pain that marks the moment that the heart wound isn't showing
but you wince below the knowledge, it was never meant to show.

To care for someone other than yourself is meritorious
the hope that someone other cares for you, as you do them
is to watch their face for features, and the warmth with which they answer
and know what you've got emerging, love could be your answer then.

War Song of the Love Bed

Teeth in my gums
he, she, it,
love – hate, hot sweat
aches,
arms, legs, flowers
upon the climbing wall
of loves tangle; I contain
as I am the sweat – wreath
and the sprung slab
bonded to you by love nightmares

I eat waste
want – nots
and on occasion, children!

Bedroom Seen

The impression on the bed
was like that of two souls,
unseen but heavy enough
to indent their presence.
The fact that she had
turned her back on him
could be noted
by the curve of her pillow
arched like a rainbow
and the support of dreams,
she had pushed away more
than his hands
to create the small space
and infinite between them.
There were hard words
in the contortion of sheets,
wish, want, or need at dream time
passing years in the activity of fluff
and sleeping thoughts.
Here for so many years
night had always been starless,
dark and silent as the grave
for which they seemed to be practised,
each would rise with age
more often than they once had done
for one reason or another.
It had crossed his mind many times
whilst waiting for something to happen,
but knowing it wouldn't,
that real death, that absence of life
would be like this
but would stop the heat
and hunger
of who listened, lied, and lay alongside.

The Water Babies

In the waters of conception before my time
in the eternity of the infinite of mind
there were two of us who swam together,
he and I, I thought, talked to him,
and he along the same line of thought he talked with I,
two souls at play within one heart.

Some times of a stillness there's his voice
I hear it now asking where I went
we were parted from each other in the swim
he became a feature of myself
one moment he was there but I had grown
two souls at play within one heart.

He often asks about the world of men
a world he hears and visualises through me
I carry him in the space next to my heart
and we share the ills of fortune
and the rise and fall, the aches and pleasures
two souls at play within one heart.

I can just remember, that before my being
I saw him briefly and he was very small
transparent as the best of beings
should be, he disappeared in the flow
of expectancy, I hope to God I brought him through with me!
Two souls at play within one heart.

I was told about him, how he was a loss
when I began. He'd never grown
but he had swum the tides and rushes
that expectancy had planned and I hold him
by my heart and keep the silence of our time

I am a man, he is my conscience and we are!
Two souls at play within one heart.

I am told I was to be twin,
there were two of me, him
and him, one of us came through
I and I which soul speaks for me.
Was he absorbed by me
or what I see is what he shares with me?

....

The concept of two becoming one
a contractual unity of self souls
sailed by us unlooked for unschooled
in the swim of things, exits and entrances.
Sometimes I catch a random thought
freed upon expression, singular
in the stream of things,
like a phantom, a presence
run off against the clock, in no time at all,
the ache of an instant, gone the next.
the haunting waited for, just the awareness
the ache of an impression, a bend in the light.,
an instance of open wound
there? Here? Where? An imagined shape?
Shadow? Form?
Two souls at play within one heart.

Enclosed within the waters at the beginning
of our world we took shape
and relationship locked us in to an ocean,

of ever growth and evolving, pushing back
the walls of our containment, stretching
their elasticity to make more room
for each other the waters were warm
and inviting our staying,
then we had not the grounding knowledge
of death, disappearance or amalgamation,
or absorption.
Two souls at play within one heart

Absorbed in myself and a shared joy
I was happily unaware that while I grew
his size had remained static stunted,
it was only when I hugged him in a handful
that difference struck us before the eyes,
and the cavities of recall. So absorbed were we
 in us we failed to see the forging of difference. I
no long held his hand but stood him on my palm,
this twin, now little brother smaller
that even my comforting smile.
Two souls at play within one heart.

Time elapsed communications of our enclosure
slowed and slipped away, I had no wish to dominate
and held my tongue and he at a loss
asked questions only of himself.
I grew and petted him and learnt to look
without words, as he asked the something of a why,
He gained anger and saw himself as less than nothing,
my talking to him was mainly to myself, he kicked,
he struck out against the walls that held us in and I
watched until mine was all the space.
Two souls at play within one heart.

Somewhere in time he was seen by the watchers
during our days of play. In the beginning we played
and I shared the time
he had been given time. Nearing the end of our enclosure
loneliness swept over me, I swam about and he was nowhere,
I could find him nowhere, in those days I learned
loneliness and I feared and fretted,
for him more so when I thought perhaps?
I had absorbed him
and this is still a recurring thought, even now?
I am set to argue with myself. Even the thought
that he simply passed away and set me to re-seek these memories
and that's when my thoughts weigh
Two souls at play within one heart.

Since that time there is a weight to my shoulders
there is nothing there though he is.

02/08/21 and 10/8/2021

But....it's True!

She offered me all and everything,
her body and her mind
on the first evening we ever shared
together, on our own
and together alone the dark lady
of my lines.

As my Eve she held out the apple
in her palm "the should nots"
of fears, coming on like the dream
of a schoolboy, feline
and slinky my dark lady
steered.

Her eyes repeated the wanting
her lips spoke acquiescently
she lifted my hands to a holding,
placed them there
saying all without words
to me.

Prior to this, a love had touched me
without the animal hands
of a lusting, A first love
now found love to be wanting
without the clamour of flesh
that expands.

Open handed I played the gallant,
missed the chance, refused
the child of fancy, weighed
a future, thought it fair
to leave and let our hunger
hang me.

Weighed a breast against time
and motion, explained myself
as best I shared, saw confusion,
controlled explosion, silenced
could not do what I would
not dare.

Demise of moment high in tension
female rush fell away, lost
the action, the conception, sigh
and speech in disarray, I said
I loved her, but would not
commit this way.

I could not tell, but from that moment
the child between us, "that
might have been", gathered
room and grew enormous
gestating correctly by the calendar
to push me out nine months later.

Voices of Spring

Voices of spring
twist of fate
love of fancy,
she talks and
he talks to her but
she is lost to him,
seeing in him
what she would like to see in him,
her head carries the brain of a sergeant-major
"I'll make a man of you" believing
he has not been broken before. Inwardly she smiles.
He is still talking to himself
When she says "Pardon?"

He is a Hairdresser to Ladies
(Pippa's father)

He is a hairdresser to Ladies,
short and with a stoop,
comes, he says,
from the weight of other people's worries:
Does what other men stand and stare
and wish to do,
run his fingers through a multitude of tresses,
caressing each as each owner vainly
opens her mouth
to expose herself to him.

His hands are shop soiled,
rough cut, parched,
and cracked,
continually in and out of water
their natural oils no longer shield.

He works his day fully,
Manfully
    -   but he smells nice.

Touches of Love:

Of Things That Were

Once the night that I knew, held her,
absorbed my face so many times.
        Kissed,
and felt her cool air boil.
            Rouge and flame.
Bright, loved
the world which I encompassed,
conquered gently, to map her face
to the stars,
        that broke my frame.   *(Written April 1967)*

With no word spoken,
sealed only in the sacred
exchange of breath,
did we inhabit,
each other.   *(Written March 2019)*

Epilogue to the Affair

So needs be the bitter taste
and the magic slowly gone,
and I realise, how in her eyes
a death, our loving looked upon.

Young, we were in season
and as such, it was our time,
losing heat, Autumn
extinguished fired twine.

Having said how, by word of mouth
in kissed simplicity,
the breath between our bodies froze,
closing she from me,

Now my skull full of minus waste
and disappearing tricks,
cannot hold against the cold
patch, she witch-like pricks.   *(Written January 1968)*

These three verses were originally longer individual poems of an emotional content, and I brought extracts of them together as one poem.

Working Script

The summer sun is over-clouded
a haze has settled in for now,
the air is heavy and unmoving,
evening enters through the flowers.
A droning bee disturbs the silence
picking ways between the stems.
He chews a stalk and stares at nothing
she cries a lot and straightens hems.

The scene is so much like a movie
the love and lust that is-as-one,
the innocence behind the picture
is misconstrued by everyone.
And they read it in the novels,
and they see it on their screens
and these are not the lines of knowledge,
these are those that lie between.

And the scene shifts to a couple
weather-worn and mapped with age,
standing mellow, 'twining fingers
like the words they'd wished they'd said.
He took a road that cost a lifetime,
she married some else instead,
in the meeting of true minds friend,
ills the love that takes to bed.

And the picture lifts its focus
panning out along the road
closing in on the horizon,
and there it lets the light explode.

On My Seventieth Birthday
(May 2nd 2016)

To my three score years
and ten, none of which will come again
I'd ask to add (like Moses) at least
fifty more to tell our stories,
and to lay the lore.

To spin the tales my time
has gained, and explain the journeys
as I've had them explained,
to laugh with all and harvest tears
across the knowledge of timeless years.

To be the child inside the man
and feast on words, because I am
all hugs and heart, and hearing speech
and holding eyes by eye-light teach
what words can't say that emotions reach.

I do not have to reel around
to know behind me holding ground
the generations of my holy tongue
have told as sacred every tale begun,
connecting through a thousand tongues
to one conveyed by us in fired night
or under the sun, that held the telling time
as Eden's place and brought its moment
as a veil of grace.*

A breath of silence and all ears
this man of earth his earthing nears
but having learnt to tell and told
forever young the story blooms,
and only its time grows old.

- *Nachman of Bratislav's Tikkun (Shards) philosophical concept (on Storytelling and what the Storyteller can achieve) was an idea that I reached totally independently before my Folklore work touched on this Chassidic Rabbi's ideas. I have carried this perspective since I was a teenager.*

- *At its simplest the idea explain in Tikkun (Shards) suggests that when man was thrown out of Eden and the gates were locked against him, the angel given the responsibility for this also shattered the memory's illusion of a Paradise. But the Almighty creator gave individual souls the gift of storytelling. A gift that lifts its engrossed listeners out of their every day existence into a state and world as near to ethereal Paradise as can be achieved in the mind.*

The Shaman's Dance

From cavalry units to airborne militia,
blue to the khaki and green;
from the long knives to short arms,
machine guns and mayhem,
Attack! and the purpose of screams.
Curious, the twists and the fantails of history
That one man should take on the lead
And stealing the breath through the teeth of his enemies
Be the one name to carry their deeds.

"One who yawns"* was the label they laughingly gave
to a legend some say never slept,
Disguised as the darkness
None spoke if they saw him
As through circling armies he crept.
The steel in his hand was a star shine and lighting
Its silence descending with fate,
He trusted to no one who had trusted too many
In holding his peoples' estate.

As the wind cut the width of the desert
He walked between armies unseen.
His darkness gave horse soldiers nightmares
His war was to save what had been.

He rode with 'rough riders' through New York,
An old man who carried the flag,
Teddy Roosevelt gave him a diamond
And called him the country's Grand-dad.
He gained no peace as an older world changed
But they threw out his name to the fore
And men'd follow him down into Hades -
that's what a good leader's born for.

The set of his eyes in a picture
speaks louder than the hands or the man.
He sees and gives nothing but silence
a death weight like the gun in his hand.
Angered by all of the lying
He poses as they wanted him to
but he knows that they are still frightened
by what magic he as a shaman can do.

The world was at war when a sergeant
in skies that merged this world with the next
in briefing the men to go forward
calming the tense and perplexed.
Had a young man turn and say "Sarge
I'm scared in the best movie fashion
But unlike the movies these are my qualms!"
"Throw out his name as you step from the plane.
Look for his face in the clouds
Follow him down to the ground -
There on your toes use friends and know foes -
Move in his mystery give 'em a lesson in history.
Green light! And go! Yell Geronimo!!!"

His was the name on the edge of the abyss
The bridge under blindness through fear,
It was he over chasms led men out of darkness,
The small man with the height of the seer.
And today we have turned his name sacred*
Saying it three times to carry a charge
And in killing his enemies' enemy
We have written his name again large.

*"One who yawns" was the birth name for Geronimo.
It was announced on the 5 o'clock news of the BBC on 27/12/2011 that the American unit which had killed Bin Laden and destroyed his headquarters, had at the start of their final assault yelled "Geronimo" three times as they ran forward.*

Lizzie Strade
(A paraphrase of 'The Lysistrata' by Aristophanes
in music hall monologue form)

I'll tell you of an ancient Greek
Her name was Lizzie Strade,
A regular prim and proper miss
Whose marriage had decayed,
Not for want of trying
But with a husband at the wars
She never had him long enough
To enjoy what he was for.

Now love was all in Lizzie's life
Whatever people say
But every time her man returned
He was just too tired to play.
The situation irked her
And she sought for its resolve
When she saw just how around the wars
The life she had revolved.

She sent to Asia Minor
And the city states of Greece
To see which other women there
Agreed her terms for peace -
That they should stand alluringly
To tease but not be touched
'til all the men their warring end
That they their favours dutched.

She told the Grecian populace
"War doesn't make a man!
To raise a spear and don a shield
You only need a hand!

But you come back for children
And expect us to amuse -
To help you wean your sons for war!
-Your daughters to be used!

Cessation of hostilities
On every single front-
An end to war forever more -
For it's we women bear the brunt!"
The men at Athens agonised
But they couldn't stand the strain,
Their hopes rose up before them
And they had to think again.

So ladies if you've had enough
Of war and wars alarms
And the eunuchs out in politics
Make of your men demands -
Talk to him quite slowly
And as the penny sinks -
Make your appeal specifically
To the thing with which he thinks!

Cabaret Song

Two little girls in an empty schoolroom
skipping rope with time in mind.
"What would you give to know the future?
What would you know if you had a mind?"
"Half o' me sweets and a dream to follow,
who'll be the one that I would wed,
turn me around and turn me over –
give me a world in the man ahead".

Same two girls on a summer morning
Sunday white and worldly brides
turning the rope until it tightens,
swearing to tell what the future hides.
"Keep in touch though seas asunder".
"Tell me how you make your bed!"
"Turn me around and turn me over –
give me a world in the man ahead".

One little girl like a duck to water,
one little girl like a sinking stone,
one little girl with a home and children,
one little girl left on her own.
First he kissed her, then he cussed her –
then the clouts about the head
turned her around and turned her over –
gave her the world of the man ahead.

Turning the rope the time is passing
putting her back upon her feet –
passing a children's playground one day

who but her old friend should she meet.
"There's someone who says he loves me,
more than all the space in bed,
' turns me around and turns me over –
gives me a world in the man ahead.

One little girl plays house to a husband,
one little girl has a happy home,
two little girls have a wealth of children –
sharing a man who is seldom home.
Neither asks the other questions,
thoughts are crossed but left unsaid
'would turn them around and turn them over –
given the man in the world ahead!

Two little girls in an empty schoolroom
skipping rope with time in mind.
"What would you give to know the future?
What would you know if you had the mind?'
"Half o' me sweets and a dream to follow,
who'll be the one that I would wed,
turn me around and turn me over –
give me a world in the man ahead".

Gurney at the Words

Music's soul to touching words,
midnight walker on the road to home;
so many friends, yet so all alone,
so full of sights of war and songs of love.
He tried to lift above the commonplace
                on English tongues
the native that was Summer's sun
as airy and observed as living life.

Gurney at the words we can feel the pain you freed,
sense your comet's burning seed to set itself
                        upon the charted sky.
Night alight and high, but only now we come to you
like drifting clouds across the moon, to listen
                as you tell us what you saw.

Whitman's words upon his lips,
a Bach chorale and then the hedgers craft,
he sifted each until he knew its staff
and always there were clouds and coloured skies
looking through his eyes we can see
                the storms that raged;
the forming mists upon those darkening days,
where gurning* at the words was Ivor's soul.

Crickley Hill and Gloucester town
he walked them up and he had walked them round,
he knew the docks when they were full of sound
And daily to the tale things broke his heart
tearing him apart

arguments inside his head
he couldn't hold a job, instead
the poems that he wrote were home and heart.

Gurney at the words, maddened by the lack of time
To spin the line from mind to mind
              Whilst writing out the same in music staves.
But as a man behaves, so the knots of reasoned thought
Tighten 'til they're so distraught there's nothing left
                      but dying in the dark,
Gassed and girl-less to the grave.
On a June night I can hear him breathe
I can make it so that I believe
The soldier from the wars is coming home.
Home to turmot-hoe, bargain,
              and the winding ways
with the insight of those Cotswold days
and the pleasure it would be to hear him read.

Gurney at the words – this is just a poorish thanks
For sharing with us season's banks and rank and file
                 With men who went to war,
And a whole lot more, of earth and time and khaki hue,
There was a man – that man was you, and you are all
                    the songs we ever sing.

  An old word meaning to pull a twisted face.

Ivor Gurney's centenary 28/8/90
A brilliant poet still relatively unknown in this country.

With Apologies to William Allingham

Up the airy mountain
    Down the rushy glen
We daren't go a hunting
    Abominable snowmen
And for why are they abominable?
    For them we've never seen,
We've only seen their footprints
    Which tell us where they've been.

In the Himalayan foothills
    Some are said to feel at home
For there they can take long walks
    And philosophise alone.
Some have claimed to have seen climbers
    But are pooh-poohed round the twist
For every little Yeti knows,
    Humans don't exist.

Nightmare

"Drop dead!" he shrieks
and his brain falls out.

His mind implodes on the ether
percussing his eyes
in sharp hammer shafts
of sickening fluorescence;
forcing them upward, inward
upon his scrambled patterns
shattered thought……
as sonic aurori
scream hell down his ears
and reeking years of curdled sweat
the clinging sheets remember.

Grasping air
as if something of new value
he shrieks "God!"
……..and goes under.

I Wake

I wake in the grey light morning
a ghost of thoughts and dreams,
tired from a nightly journey
wondering where I've been -
across a space of absences
soully shapeless and purely mind,
I sought amongst the sleepers
for one I could not find,
where here no names much matter
and the thoughtless are the blind.
This journey I make every night
across the timeless length of lives
all mine and everlasting,
not sure of what I'll find,
the vibes of some familiar breath,
an aging heart like mine,
the echo of a hanging sigh,
the lost love of a lie.
Is this what makes an angel,
a presence felt and gone.
A surveyor of that other world,
as ethereal as a song?

Tisha B' AV.
(The 9th Day of The Jewish month of Av)
(The scene of this piece was the old Nelson Street Synagogue, Whitechapel, in East London, in the mid 1960's.)

Like a homing exile seeking sanctuary, I have come back
to one moment, for the light of one evening, of one time,
if only in thought without question,
hearing a hollow echo off ringing walls
and the slow shuffle of soft shoes
on bare wooden floorboards, the sound of old men
with age creaks, moaning, sighing, seating themselves with relief
on those bare boards as close to the ground
as bodily allowed. Each in his turn smiles, jokes, *"acchs"*
at the thought he has to rise again.

In a dot dash circle of straightened spines, legs folded,
legs stretched one way or another they begin now
as they did then, now as they have always done
as I remember. Their singsong sobbing enhances
the stillness around me. The old poet beside me
licks his forefinger to collect a page, the sound of which
is like a knife slicing through air as the paper buckles
and turns, to lie under that fingerbrushing - the words.
Crossed legged, head bent over the concerning text,
I see him, my teacher, amid the rubble of stone.

I drift and they are not old, they are ancients I know,
souls I have never met but have known in time -
to each I put a name, that name is out of date.
They wail and beat their hearts, my cheeks are wet
and I am crying, I have buried my heart in the page
amid the text of my people's ancient tongue.

What is it that has torn the heart out of us, that we sit
stirring a fog of dust off the floorboards, ashes in the mind
where our fathers and grandfathers called for home
in those days when we reached these shores of our journey.

The shadows lengthen and a shudder creeps along
the growing chill, now the sunlit dust haunts
like frozen breath inanimately hanging
in time to dissipate. I note the brickwork shines
a sheen that falls away to rubble that weeps pebbles.
Coughs and voices, figments in the light of time,
never really full of hearts that filled in the space
intoning lamentations. Old voices extol each other,
the nasal whine of why and for what reason
has the man of God screaming down the desolate years.

Hardly harmonies, more dissonances, louder almost
in attempts to outdo each other, they vocalise
colourlessly in a mass of tortured emotion,
metronomic measures beaten fist on broken heart
these are the men who were there every time.
As I was! I am that I am! And I look into their faces,
recalling each in his turn with an unlined face centuries before -
the first time, the second time, each time led away
to forget. But we could not forget time and time again,
if I am not for my own – who is for me and when?

Here again we sit mourning the presence of the past,
ghosting ourselves as in a hall of mirrors
where what reflects us is real enough, but
without the depth of time each instance ages us.
Here again we sit backs to the wall beside the City Gate,
Storytellers of eternal time, translating words

into actions, nailing painful regrets into our hearts,
dust to dust, how many times, when breathing
have we consumed ourselves over centuries,
man, rock, rubble, dust, and earth in the end we will fill a space.

Every little while my teacher pulls away from his page
turns to me, observes, says nothing but smiles,
returns his concentration to the past, woken out of words
I look up as he looks down, time taken to communicate
between the generations something exchanged, the unsaid
said. I am here, there and in a hundred other places,
memory runs through my veins, a shadow tells me
it is still not time enough – I bow my head to the text
and narrow my sight, before time is the past, around me
is the moment, in the rubble and dust awaits tomorrow.

The singsong stills, and within minutes broken, dies away
carried in time's temples of the mind, reminding
that neither story or journey have been concluded.
Speechlessly with nods and knowing looks,
smiles and downcast eyes, shoulders rounded
by the centuries' pull of memories' weight, in this
creening lament and the reality in the dust
of all things that live, these masters rise slowly
as though their aged tears polish stone, built a city,
as my old teacher and I will discuss and dispel the darkened night.

Blackbury Castle (1)

Strange no birds. There are
beyond the wall, the dyke and the road
But here, where too many trees have taken,
None. And here meandering

Its earthen parapet,
A shaven path in the grass
Rounds its broken circuit
About the silence like the low sun.

That foxy slips the green cover
with russet light in sharp relief.
Who was the last to walk here
in featherlight to nothingness, in such disturbing truancy?

In the daybright dimlight under the wall,
Back against the bank
Seated on the cold grass
I whistled for effect and heard the flat sound die.

Blackbury Castle (2)

Once there was a girl,
as dark as the days appeared that she turned from me,
who wished I would have the woman of her
in such a place.

It would be early, half light,
half night, dewy the wet grass
star struck breaking under her back,
who wished the sole sound surrounding,

To be that of her breath alive
and in the fashion of folksong to wear her skirt
sky high above the knee and unafraid.
And so she toed her tongue flexing,

The image of me, my hair spring triggered by her
taste for orange cream perfume
through my nose, and out of her head
where as artist she was as full of pictures.

I was aware of bodies when in my mind I came here
and saw this place in the time allotted, but she is not here,
not now. She who wished has her own circa
its high banks and songless trees, and I am in there somewhere.

Why Poetry?

Of course, I can be as cheap
and nasty in a strident tongue or
as fluently complementary
with the chisel of a pen. Foul
or fair, I am as plain as I am
in your face.
You pick me up and colouring
thought of a moment you read me
as I am, and as I am
out to disturb you, to catch a change
of expression, the thought is here.
You will remember my name
these days my ethnicity too.
Listen to what I say again and again.

To The Storytellers

Put the book down! Picture
the mind, the eyes have it, the features
convey. Don't look for narrative
along the life lines in the flatlands of your hands,
experience puts them there -
like the tale that wears your face.
Create and extend in the bowl of your fingers
the reach of your insight
and the stream of its light,
lay out endeavour, diversion and resolve,
humour and pathos – heartbreak and love
song. Commit to expression that
which cannot be seen – but sensed
in an intake of breathing -
the grasp of a gasp,
the connection of thought. The transmission
of image and its reception as viewed.

Face on and lip kissing each word
that you utter, the essence of you in the story
you form – whether it's yours
or the adventure of others
let it hang in the air, before
you pause for applause.

Printed in Great Britain
by Amazon